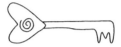

Dedicated to all the Angels
in my world

with special thanks to
Brian Andreas for his StoryPeople
quotes sprinkled throughout this story.

Robert Keep Believing
the miracle is in you!
Sonia 11/15

The Miracle Keys

Unlocking the Mysteries
to a Life of Deep Happiness
and Lasting Abundance

Project Management by Pottenger Press
For information: PottengerPress.com

ISBN 978-0-9969037-0-7

Printed in the United States of America

Contents

A DREAM AND A VISION

*How I started
believing in miracles.*

In my dream, the angel shrugged
& said,

If we fail this time,
it will be a failure of imagination

& then she placed the world
gently in the palm of my hand.

Brian Andreas

A Dream and A Vision

The first time I met her, it was in a dream. I'm not an avid dreamer, so her visit made quite an impression. She waltzed right in, brushed my mind with images I could never forget, and gave me a whole new world.

She led me to a room that at first seemed too bright for my eyes. But something in the way she pulled me forward prompted me to take another look. The mirrored walls reflected a million tiny prisms of diamond light. The ceiling, if it was even there, appeared as an endless expanse of night sky.

I could have easily gotten lost in the shine, but the Angel took my hand and guided me to take my place at the perfectly round sapphire blue table in the middle of the room.

Gazing into the depths was like nothing I'd ever experienced—an immersion in crystal waters and star-encrusted sky swirling together into infinity. A merging of heaven and earth...new constellation beyond light and sound...all colors of life erupting with sensations that blasted my sense of form and left me basking in a vast puddle of immaculate Love.

That might have been enough for me, but she wasn't finished.

Just as I was ready to fall completely into the brilliant expanse before me, she started to speak. It wasn't in a language I understood at first, so it's taken me years to piece together the puzzle she laid before me.

But what she showed me that night has stayed with me, directing the trajectory of my life.

When I awoke from the dream, what I remembered most was a feeling of deep peace, and a vision.

The vision was of a group of women gathered around a large table, with an endless supply of money flowing in. Our job was simply to send out the money in ways that would create joy.

Not having had much experience with the metaphor of dreams, I took this quite literally and created The Abundance Angels Project, a group of earth angels focused on creating random acts of abundance for our community.

The Abundance Angels group lasted a short while, but not as long as the dream.

That dream stayed with me as I followed my passion over the years, seeking the essence of the seed vision so I could nurture it to life.

Looking back, I realize I was attempting to re-create the sense of total freedom and limitless abundance I felt standing in that dream room.

It's taken years to unlock the deeper Message—along with a couple more visits from the Angel.

This is a story about our conversation.

PART I

CONVERSATION WITH AN ANGEL

It all began with a dream.

The Angel

She came back years later, after I had wandered through cycles of Earth, at times exhausted from the pain of it—more often amazed at the sheer beauty that lives here.

She came after I had explored the outer edges of consciousness, awakening to a deeper knowing of my own divinity...of yours too.

She came when I was ready to listen to the parts of the Message I had missed during her first visit.

She brought with her five assistants, whom I later named, The Keepers.

They came when I was getting just a little too comfortable with my life, just as I had begun to give up on that initial spark and was starting to settle for someone else's dream.

I was ushered, once again, into the Diamond Light room. We stood around the sapphire table, me slightly trembling from the majesty before me; they, gazing calmly and patiently ahead, as if they had all the time in the world.

A part of me realized that they did.

As we stood together in this timeless embrace, I returned to that place of immaculate, iridescent Love that seemed to enter from everywhere at once. It flowed through my veins, flooded my bones, and turned my form to liquid Light.

After awhile, I sensed they were waiting for me to speak.

For a few minutes—perhaps an eternity—my mind was so blank I couldn't even remember how to form letters into words.

Then slowly a question began to form, and I felt them understand before my mind had even grasped what my heart was yearning to know.

What am I to do, now that I've felt this Great Love?

A simple inquiry, yet one that seems to arise often as we 'awaken' and begin to know something beyond the ordinary.

How can one possibly go about 'normal' life after experiencing such an exquisite taste of Absolute Love?

"You might say this is the whole point," said the Angel, once again reading my mind.

"You are here to bring this divine Love to earth, and to create your own heaven here.

As you learn to access what you've experienced in your daily life, you'll find a deeper and more lasting happiness. You'll also discover your true destiny.

Let us remind you of the Way."

Most people don't know

there are angels

whose only job is to make sure

you don't get too comfortable

& fall asleep & miss your life.

Brian Andreas

The Keepers and the Keys

The Angel turned to the Keepers. I had almost forgotten they were there; they were shimmering so brightly and blending together so completely. Even now, after meeting each One, I can see how their connectedness can make them appear as mirages of one another.

When the Angel nodded, one of the Keepers stepped into more vivid form, moving forward until she stood directly before me.

As she took my hand in hers, I felt something inside me unlock, as if a secret compartment had sprung wide open after years of being stuck partially closed.

"Yes," she nodded. "This is what we are here to show you. Now just close your eyes so I can deliver the first of the hidden keys."

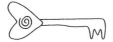

Images entered my mind almost faster than I could grasp. Years of partially understood truths flashed before me.

I could see the places where I had misunderstood—or been unprepared to receive—the fullness of those experiences.

But rather than feeling a slight bit of regret for the limited way my life had been until now, all I felt was utter amazement.

As I felt the past dissolve...as I stood in total acceptance of what had been...as I merged willingly and irrevocably with the energetic current I felt pass through my body and mind...all I felt was complete peace and endless freedom.

I knew deep in my heart that everything I had experienced in my life until now, and everything that would pass through my life in the future, was to be simply returned to God. There is nothing to cling to, no holding on.

Like a river moving through the landscape of my life, all parts of the journey washing through in one continuous flow.

The Keeper moved back to her place in the circle.

"Well done," spoke the Angel. "You have experienced the first Key. Forgiveness will unlock your destiny and set you free."

Forgive...and Keep Forgiving

*M*y mind entered. "But I thought forgiveness had to do with pardoning another for some wrongful act," my mouth inelegantly sputtered.

The Angel smiled. "Perhaps there is nobody and nothing to forgive, but simply that everything is *for* the *giving*."

She paused to let that sink in, and then continued. "When we accept what IS, seeing everything as part of an undivided whole, we become more fully present and aware of what is happening right now.

As we let go of worry about what *might* happen in the next moment, we can pay closer attention to this one."

This is what I had experienced—a total freeing of my mind to attend to this moment. No more being caught in some lingering energy from the past, or potential from the future.

I thought about how much of my time I spend thinking of what has just happened, or wondering at what is about to happen, which actually leaves very little of my attention available to focus on what is happening in this very moment.

Even now I found myself thinking about how most people consider 'forgiveness' to be something we DO rather than a way we can choose to BE.

"I forgive you, and now that I have forgiven you, everything will be ok," ...or, "I forgive you for what you have done, and I forgive myself for being caught up by it," ...or even, "I ask God to forgive you (though I may never-ever-ever forget ;-)."

When we think we must *act* in forgiveness, the ego is in charge. Forgiveness is what we must *do* to resolve something that is incomplete, a way to release our mind from obsessing over what someone has done to us.

When forgiveness becomes an internal act that must be taken, it can easily turn into a moral stance that keeps us stuck in separation.

But true forgiveness is so much more.

Forgiveness is stepping into arms of grace, bowing our heads, and allowing everything to pass through without attachment. Which is virtually impossible while we live in a body.

Yet this is the first sacred Key. Attach to nothing. Give everything. Everything is for giving—not for keeping.

When we embrace forgiveness as a way of *being*, it is more like standing in a river, accepting that we are part of the flowing waters rather than one of the rocks.

Forgiveness becomes an art, a beautiful dance with the Divine that requires no apology—so long as we remember who is leading the Dance!

The Angel closed her eyes, and emitted a small sigh. "We'll come back to this again," she said. "Again, and again, and again."

I laughed. And laughed, and laughed, and laughed.

"Of course we will!" I gasped. "This is obviously not something even an Awake Being can *Do* simply once and be *Done*."

What on earth were we thinking?

I laughed some more.

I used to wait for a sign, she said,

before I did anything.

Then one night I had a dream

& an angel in black tights came to me & said, you can start
any time now, & then I asked, is this a sign?

& the angel started laughing

& I woke up.

Now, I think the whole world

is filled with signs, but if there's no laughter,

I know they're not for me...

Brian Andreas

Ahhhhhh. It's Good to Laugh.

*S*o, what's next?

"You're already there," laughed the second Keeper as she waltzed up to me and took my hand. "This earth life is an intricate dance, and laughter is just about the only way you'll ever survive it."

Notice that we're not going to number these Keys, since that might imply some order of importance. They are ALL equally significant; you just need to know when to use each one. Most often, you'll want to use them all at once."

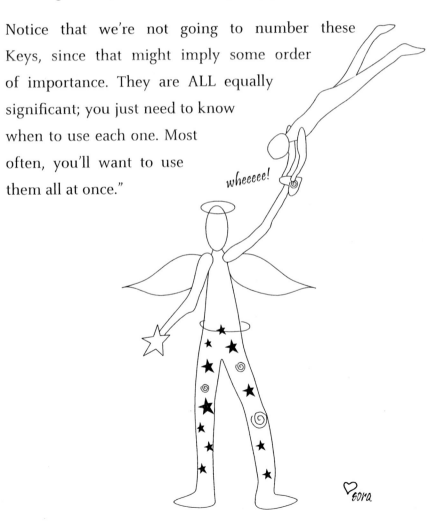

wheeeee!

♡ sara

"Simultaneous Unlocking. Hahahahaha!"

The Keeper of Laughter is quite delighted with herself, it seems.

I just stared at her, my mind blank. She stared back, and before long we were locked in one of those childhood games where the first to blink loses. Of course I was the one.

She laughed.

"Don't worry if you forget this key every once in awhile. You had it as a child, but lost it somewhere in your teens when you were trying to make an impression. Most adults seem to misplace this key as they go about the business of being 'grown up'. When they start trying to earn a living and all that."

I grinned and told her I'd read about that somewhere.

We kept up the banter for a while longer, and I laughed so enthusiastically that tears began streaming down my face.

But then I started to ponder some of the less amusing parts of life, and apparently my face showed signs of confusion.

My laughter had been genuine, and I definitely felt something deeper unlock in those moments of glee. But I started to feel a bit self-conscious, and then a little guilty at having so much fun when there are so many serious problems in the world.

"You're taking this all much too seriously," said the Keeper of Laughter.

"But, how can I be anything *but* serious when there is so much to be serious about?" I replied.

Ahhhhh, she sighed. "It's true, there is much sadness here, and strife. Most humans don't have a clue how to avoid it. And some of it IS, indeed, a necessary part of this Earth experience you have chosen.

But you've seen how some humans will rise above the difficulties and manage to thrive in the midst of chaos and suffering.

You've seen the effects of walking through pain with an open heart.

You've seen how laughter can erase the lines of despair that separate and keep you in the cage of your own seriosity."

I smiled. Seriosity is a word I invented to remind myself to play. Curiosity may have killed a cat (though I don't think so). But seriosity is bound to kill the joy that naturally arises as we connect with the heart of life.

So even if we're not meant to laugh at many parts of life, laughter can ease the constriction that comes when life seems to be falling apart around us.

"It's as good a way as any to wake up laughing," the Keeper of Laughter whispered as she danced back to her place in the circle.

Angel Break

"*I* can see you're starting to doubt your ability to learn these Keys, but please remember that I wouldn't have brought you here if you didn't already possess everything you need."

My eyes closed as I tried to believe what she was saying. She listened for a moment before continuing to speak, as if she were giving the words room to grow.

"Within you is a divine Seed, and every choice you make will either nourish the Seed, coaxing it to grow, or leave it dormant inside.

The Seed will always be there. Every human has one, though many seeds remain buried for lifetimes, undernourished and kept in the dark.

The essential Seed of your being needs Light to grow."

I nodded my head. I've worked hard to keep cultivating my own divine seed and have sometimes felt exhausted from all that effort.

The Angel peered at me with her luminous eyes. I seemed to be missing something.

"Perhaps you could simply *open* to the Light and allow your Seed to find nourishment there."

I felt a click as another lock sprung open.

I nodded again, but this time it was my heart that knew the Answer.

I saw a vision of myself sitting in a room, alone and in the dark, trying so hard to connect with the inner light I knew was inside.

Then suddenly, the room was flooded with light, as though someone had flipped a switch. My body merged with the light around me, and I became a part of what was already there.

I laughed at the image of my body sitting with such intense concentration as I tried to squeeze the light out. In that moment, I realized the error of what I had previously thought.

I had somehow believed I had to work hard to become something different, rather than allowing what I already am to naturally shine.

I wondered what this had to do with finding happiness.

"When you stop seeking for happiness outside of you—when you begin to realize that what you seek is within—true happiness becomes possible."

"But that is only the beginning," said the third Keeper, flowing elegantly from her place at the table to take my hand.

"Let us take a look into the Art of Believing."

Why do we believe stuff that's not true?

he said & I said

because it's easier than admitting we don't know.

Which is a lot closer to reality...

Brian Andreas

Believe...and Let Go of Beliefs

I considered what the Keeper said about the *Art of Believing*. I had quite a few questions about what to believe at all.

In fact, it seems like every time I begin to believe one thing, I find almost the opposite can also be true.

"Does happiness have something to do with choosing what to believe and then finding a way to keep believing no matter what?" I asked.

"Well, yes and no," replied the Keeper.

"Part of your task is to *stop* believing what you've learned that is keeping you from fully believing *in* yourself, which might have to do with believing too much *about* yourself, keeping you too focused *on* yourself.

It can be a bit intricate, when you come right down to it."

"I see." I replied. Though, to be honest, I wasn't quite sure I was seeing anything clearly at all.

I tried from another angle. "Are you indicating there are different kinds of beliefs, some more harmful than helpful?" I asked.

The Angel smiled. "Of course. It's just a matter of which part of you is doing the believing."

I was beginning to understand. When our mind attaches to a belief—especially one it has picked up from someone else—there's a tendency to turn that belief into some kind of judgment.

On the other hand, when our heart believes in something completely, it nourishes the divine Seed inside, flooding it with light so it can continue to grow.

"Exactly," said the Keeper of Beliefs. (All the Keepers seem to be really good at mind reading.)

"Belief of the heart is an absolutely essential nutrient for a joyful life, while beliefs of the mind can plant a lot of weeds that crowd the divine Seed and keep it from growing.

Even the beliefs that appear nourishing can sometimes get in your way."

My mind wasn't entirely ready for this. *How could a positive belief be considered a weed?*

The Keeper noticed my doubt and tried to explain. "When you become too attached to *thinking* something is true, you may miss the heart's *knowing*. What may be true for one person is seldom right for another.

This is why we call it the Art of Believing. It begins in the HeArt."

I heard the Keeper of Laughter giggling in the background.

I turned to smile at her as I considered what I'd just heard. I was beginning to see why so many humans are unhappy, and how my own mind often disturbs my natural sense of peace.

I thought about how the brain wants to complicate everything, to be quite literally at the 'head'—directing the show.

I thought about how much of what we learn in our lives is 'taught' by someone else...and that we are seldom instructed to find the answers for ourselves.

I thought about how much time is spent 'unlearning' what we have picked up in the first part of our lives.

I thought so much I was starting to get a headache.

The Keeper interrupted me, winking at the others as she erased my mind and guided my hands over my heart. I felt an intense glow of light pulse from her hands through mine, and I realized that she had just given me another Key.

"Believe you have something important inside of you. And trust that life is giving you everything you need to let it shine through."

Can you prove any of the stuff you believe in?

my son asked me

& when I said that's not how belief works,

he nodded & said

that's what he thought

but he was just checking to make sure

he hadn't missed a key point...

Brian Andreas

Have Faith...and Trust the Journey

*B*elieve in what's inside of me. Trust that everything I need is here.

"This is about nourishing the divine Seed by opening to the light rather than trying to force it to grow, isn't it?" I asked nobody in particular.

The Angel turned to the Keeper who'd just infused me with such a refreshing glow of heart-full belief. I smiled appreciatively at her, and then gasped out loud as the single Keeper morphed into three before my astonished eyes.

The two emerging Keepers spoke simultaneously.

"You could say it begins with having faith. Although sometimes it is difficult to trust what is happening here on Earth, which can shake the faith of even the most avid believers."

I was feeling a bit confused again, which is hardly unexpected given what I'd just witnessed.

"What's the difference between faith and trust?" I wondered aloud.

"Well, they are sometimes used interchangeably, although in substance they are not quite the same. Like beliefs, one is a matter of heart, the other a choice of mind.

Faith, in its purest form, means choosing to trust there is something bigger at work in the universe. It means believing in God, but perhaps in a different way than some of us might have been taught.

Some will have a deep faith in God, but misunderstand the way faith is meant to work on Earth."

I assumed they were referring to the way so many wars are started in the name of God.

The Keepers continued. "Yes, faith can be a bit convoluted here. It's one of the most divisive principles of indivisibility, when you get right down to it.

It's a big topic, and there is much more we could say, but all the talking in the world cannot teach faith. As we've already said, it's another matter of heart."

I smiled and felt my heart open a bit more.

"Is it possible to have complete faith in something so invisible, and still have a hard time trusting the visible?" I asked.

The Keepers nodded their heads in unison.

"That's what forgiveness is for," said the Keeper of Forgiveness.
"That's what laughter is for," said the Keeper of Laughs.

"And that's what believing is about," said the Keeper of Beliefs. She was standing very still as her two wing-mates spoke.

I noticed the Angel smiling, and thought of how the five Keepers had blended together when I first saw them. I was beginning to see how these Keys are so very inter-connected.

At the moment, the Belief Keepers were a bit more animated than the others. It appeared they'd had this conversation before and were still finding it difficult to pin down in easy Earth language.

"Let's just say that trust is something that can elude even the most faith-full human beings.

Trust is about following a path that reveals itself to you only after you start walking. It's a weaving of the heart and mind that draws you forward, one step at a time.

It can be challenging to believe that earthly events are unfolding to bring you to your perfect place, especially when things don't happen in the way you would like.

Both faith and trust are essential to keep following the path of the soul.

Faith springs from the heart. Trust unlocks the mind.

When grounded in Faith, Trust is never blind.

F or a long time,

she flew only when she thought

no one else was watching...

Brian Andreas

Learning to Fly

I could feel the Keepers hovering, and decided to give voice to the doubt that lingered in my mind.

"It can be rather frightening to step onto a path that's not quite formed yet. How do I know I won't be stepping off a cliff?"

"Well, falling is entirely possible, isn't it?" the Keepers laughed in unison.

I must have looked startled.

"Sometimes you must take a step into the abyss. In fact, at times it's best to turn that step into a giant leap. That is, after all, the only way you'll ever learn to fly."

A part of me was shaking in my shoes while another part grew excited by the truth of what they were saying.

I was having a hard time convincing parts of my mind to let go of the doubt it had strived to build up over the years. But I felt the possibility begin to flutter up from somewhere inside my heart, and it was as if doors to a secret room had opened.

The Keepers leaned closer and peered into the dark corners of my mind, until suddenly a soft glow filled the new space inside.

As we looked together, it became clear that where I had created fear and mistrust, there was really nothing there.

As the light devoured the darkness, my doubt simply disappeared. I was left with a feeling of spaciousness, as if the whole roof had been removed and I was being given an entirely new room to live in.

I felt like dancing.

The Keepers took my hands and spun me around and around in this new expansiveness, as my mind merged with the heart's bright faith in a completely new way of believing.

I saw clearly how faith and trust are the partners that will cultivate the deeper belief necessary to take those flying leaps.

Faith opens the door to the heart, but only when we begin to Trust the path that is emerging before us can Belief give us wings.

The three Keepers wrapped their arms around one another, formed a circle, and began to glow. "I believe we're done for now, but we'll come back when you're ready."

And, with that, the three Keepers merged back into one.

She danced her way back to the circle, looking quite happy with what had just transpired.

Don't you hear it? she asked

& I shook my head no

& then she started to dance

& suddenly there was music everywhere &

it went on for a very long time

& when I finally found words

all I could say was thank you...

Brian Andreas

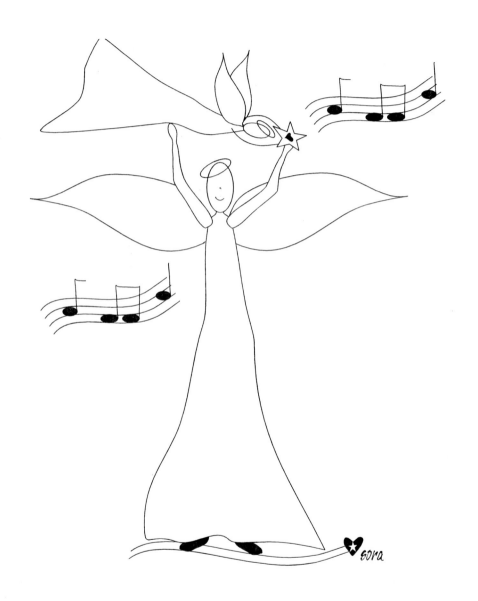

We pause for a short

intermission while you take a breath

to count your blessings.

Give Gratitude

I was sitting on the floor, having whirled with abandon until my legs could no longer hold me. At the moment, my body was a puddle of happiness, and I was aware of a shimmering glow beginning to radiate from every part of me.

Smiling in appreciation, I did my best to focus my attention on the next Keeper who was beginning to move my way.

"Ahhhhhh. So wondrous to be filled with appreciation for life, yes?"

It wasn't really a question, but I think my head gave a nod of agreement. I know my heart was nodding, vibrating like a cat in full purr mode.

There didn't seem to be appropriate words to share what I was feeling, so I settled for a satisfied smile and a grateful sigh.

The Keeper took it as a sign I was ready and began to speak.

"You're showing me that you understand this Key, perhaps more completely now than you did before. Is this true?" she asked.

I paused to consider.

"Well, it seems there's a new dimension to what I'm feeling right now. I've known how to be grateful with my mind, counting my blessings and saying thank you just about every day.

And I often feel my heart opening with great fullness of appreciation and thankfulness, especially when I connect with nature and sense the abundant blessings there.

At the moment, I seem to be experiencing each of these in a much more intense and integrated way. It's a bit like every cell in my body is humming to a great symphony, and the music can be heard across the Universe."

The Keeper gave a small nod. "Yes, it can be heard. We hear your gratitude more deeply than you will ever know."

She spoke softly, but her words pierced my heart, an arrow of truth reverberating and resounding into every part of me.

I felt a crescendo of understanding and knew she had given me another Key.

It's not enough to say the words. So many of our prayers and rituals of appreciation have become merely a dull reflection of what we've been taught to say from when we were young.

It's not enough to fill journals with long lists of what we're grateful for, although that's a good place to start.

For gratitude to be fully heard, it must be felt.

The humming grew louder. The Keeper turned to the others with a nod of appreciation, and I began to see how it's even more than this.

For gratitude to be fully heard, it must be shared.

Like most things in life, our Thanks is for Giving.

I heard a little snicker from the corner, but ignored it for now. I was onto something and didn't want to get distracted.

The Gratitude Keeper encouraged me to continue. She seemed to be deferring to me, but I knew that the music I was feeling inside was being ignited by her Presence.

The music formed into words.

When gratitude is deeply felt, it cannot help but overflow, and it's within this flow that magic happens.

The flow of gratitude becomes genuinely generous appreciation that opens hearts and creates a universal music of connection.

This is the kind of gratitude that calls the angels to sing along. And when they do, life becomes a holy symphony.

I felt a bit humble after singing those words out loud, but the Angel and the Keepers seemed to take it in stride. The quiet one whispered what they were all thinking.

"The music is always here, surrounding us—a Universal song that has been playing for all time.

It wants you to sing along. But until you listen to the deep currents of your own inner music—until you hear the song of gratitude that comes when your heart opens to embrace the entirety of who you are—you may not hear the purest notes of the Universal Song."

She paused to let that sink in.

"So this Key is not only about being grateful for the singing, but about appreciating our own part in the choir...and then being willing to sing along?"

She nodded. "Gratitude will help you sing your part with enthusiasm. It is the harmony that blends all the pieces together."

As I bowed my head, the Keeper returned to take her place in the choir.

Today there is such stillness

& gratitude

for this life that pays no attention

to what I think I want.

Brian Andreas

Be Still and Know

The room was silent. You could hear a pin drop.

I looked at the Angel, as she gazed toward the last Keeper with a look of such complete devotion that it took my breath away.

While I had not perceived any movement or sound, the Angel and all the Keepers had moved from the table and were now surrounding me, standing so close I could barely move.

After a time, I began to sense a thickening in the air, as though every molecule had been injected with some gelatinous substance.

I couldn't move. The air began to vibrate. The words formed without sound. They were in every part of me, and I was listening from somewhere outside my form, at the same time every cell paid careful attention to what was being said.

Be Still and Know.

Be Still and Know... I Am.

I Am the Sound before the Word.

I Am the Silent Music that is always here.

Be Still... and Know... I Am.

The message moved beyond and around and within, until there was nothing and everything. Time vanished and expanded.

Form turned to light, so brilliant I had to close my eyes. Yet everything at once became so clear.

I dropped to my knees in humble acceptance of the enormity of Presence surrounding and encompassing my form.

After a time, another Message began to emerge. It may have come from the Angel or any of the Keepers, though I felt it singing simultaneously from within and outside myself.

"The ultimate gift is within you.

The real miracle comes when you begin to share it with the world."

The Ultimate Gift

*Y*es, this is where the true miracle begins.

The Angel was shining more brightly than before, and when I looked down I noticed there was something a bit different about my own form as well.

We were alone in the room, and it appeared as though the starry sky had come closer. It was surrounding us, the stars glittering and glimmering (that's even more than a twinkle), and I had a feeling of being somehow inter-woven in an endless web of light.

When I asked where the Keepers had gone, the Angel just smiled.

Which is exactly when I realized they had taken up house in my heart, right where they had been all along.

I noticed that same heart was beating rather loudly. I was sure it could be heard across the sky. When I looked up, I could see that the Angel was listening too.

The heartbeat became a kind of background music that steadied me as it pulsed with what I'd just heard.

The ultimate gift is within, and the miracle comes through sharing...
The ultimate gift is within, and the miracle comes through sharing...

The ultimate Gift is within. The miracle comes through sharing.

What if this entire life is simply about giving what we have inside, rather than a never-ending journey to seek something more?

I felt the truth and simplicity of these words, at the same time I embraced their power.

Light began to radiate from inside and outside my form, infusing my heart with more Love than I had ever known.

The Angel stood beside me, extending her great Light toward mine until our radiance beamed into the night sky, a lighthouse beaconing into the dark.

I was reminded of the Diamond Light room, the feeling of expansiveness that had sparked the quest that had started this conversation, and realized that I had indeed found an Answer.

What am I to do, now that I've felt this Great Love?

I am to BE it. I am to become so full with this Love that it overflows through every part of my life and resonates into the world beyond.

This is how we create a new Earth and live our destiny...by allowing Love to flow through us in everything we do.

Giving isn't about serving for endless hours in an attempt to prove we are worthy of God's Love. It is simply allowing the limitless flow of Absolute Love that is always here to keep shining through.

This is all it's ever been about, and we only complicate it by thinking we are here to claim something for ourselves.

We stood together a few more moments gazing out at forever.

Then the Angel clasped my hand and whispered a parting message before she faded into the brilliant star-encrusted sky.

"True happiness will find YOU as you give generously from this vast universe of Love.

It won't always look like what you think, and choosing to walk the Path of Universal Love may end up taking everything you thought you had.

Your destiny is to keep opening to what has been encoded in your heart all along. Listen to the still Presence that will always be here to guide you. It will show you the path.

Then keep forgiving, laughing and giving gratitude for every part of your miraculous life.

And always keep believing."

A shimmer of a smile traveled through my body as I thought back to that first dream and embraced what it had been trying to teach me.

The limitless flow of God's Love is always here. When we learn to receive and give from within this abundance, life becomes an ongoing flow of miracles.

And, with the whole world clasped gently in my hands, I vowed to keep imagining and believing...while opening to and embracing the everyday miracles that are always here.

The End

Or is it just another Beginning?

The Angel & Keepers
(a poem)

I stand in humble grace
as each Keeper takes her place...
unlocking another part of me
within this holy embrace.

Forgiveness flows through every part
her message deep within my heart:
the freedom comes within the giving
to every thing, a fresh new start.

Laughter dances all around me
opening my mind with a touch of glee.
Innocence is thus revealed
the inner smile to never flee.

Belief and Trust with Faith combine
to reveal the inner Gift divine.
Inner treasures unlock with these,
encouraged now to simply shine.

Gratitude then takes her place
surrounding the rest, opening space;
and here is where the choir begins
returning all to eternal grace.

Now comes Stillness, a sacred art
she brings heaven to earth, mind to heart;
weaving her deep and lasting Love
forever together, never apart.

PART II

UNLOCKING THE MYSTERIES
Putting Your Keys to Use

Pssst.

It's all about generously sharing your Gifts.

Secret #8:

This world is amazing
& you'll forget that again
& again your whole life.

But if you remember
more than you forget,
you'll be fine.

Brian Andreas

Another Dream...and a Confession

*C*aught in a different dream—this one a nightmare.

Demons are chasing me through a murky swamp, trying to pull me under as I hop from one dry piece of land to another.

Just when I think my racing heart and sweat-drenched body are going to collapse into the muck and get sucked down into a bottomless dark abyss, I see her.

The Angel is back.

She beckons me from the darkness, reminding me that I have wings and need only to spread them wide to lift myself back into the Light.

I follow her beyond the edges of the swamp into a grassy meadow decorated with just about every kind of wildflower you can imagine.

"What was that about?" I ask, trying unsuccessfully to turn my thoughts away from the nightmare. My entire body is still shaking and feeling the intense anxiety of being chased through that dark and dreary swamp.

"It was just your fears trying to catch you again, to drop you back into the illusion."

The Angel floats down to perch on the edge of a boulder, then gazes peacefully across the color-infused meadow. I take my place beside her, trembling and trying to catch my breath.

I realize that I'm feeling quite a bit of irritation toward her, even though she did just save me from being devoured by demons.

"Where have you been all these months while I've been spinning in and out of depression...feeling so lost and alone...wondering where my passion & joy have gone?"

"I've been right beside you all along. You simply forgot to invite me in."

"It's quite alright," the Angel whispers as I bow my head in regret. "This whole life is a continuous stream of remembering and forgetting. As long as you remember more than you forget, you'll find your way through whatever comes."

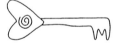

Whew.

I wrote that nightmare in present tense to remind myself what can happen when we forget to pay attention, which happens all the time.

When I initially woke from the nightmare, I knew it was an important message. We all have brilliant moments of remembering, and tremendous forces pulling us to forget.

It's so easy to get sucked into the negativity...so compelling to stay stuck rather than to keep moving in a state of grace...so common to ignore the ongoing wonder of life in favor of the crisis and chaos that is always growing around us.

So here's my confession. Even though it's natural for me to focus on the positive and miraculous, I still get caught in my own negative spin and lose track of what I know—that we shine most brightly when we are giving.

At the time of the nightmare, I had been feeling abandoned and alone, dipping in and out of depression as I considered (for the umpteenth time) what I might do to find the passion that seems to have deserted me when I hit menopause. Things that used to fire me up were failing to cause even a spark, and I seemed to be getting bored with life way more often than ever before.

I know it's fairly common, even intended, to find some level of discontent as we move through the various phases of life—it's how we keep evolving. It's possibly more intense for women as we adjust to the extreme hormonal changes of menopause, though I know many men also begin to question their sense of purpose and belonging as they grow through life.

But, honestly, I believe it's much more than discontent that many are experiencing right now.

The universe is quickening, and some of the things that used to serve as fuel are simply no longer working. Perhaps we are getting called to be more generously authentic in everything we do. Perhaps the world needs us to be more connected and conscious than ever before.

When existing structures break down, and environmental disasters strike, humans respond with more compassion and creativity than ever.

So what if every small bit of discontent, every interruption that causes us to turn inward and upward, is really just luring us to show up as the most vibrant and vital version of ourselves?

Before the nightmare startled me into paying closer attention, I had been moving in and out of dissatisfaction, but overall I was quite content with my simple, peaceful life.

But as I looked closer at the message from the dream, I understood that I've been failing to invite in the support that might open me to something even brighter.

I began to realize that I'd gotten a bit lazy with my life, and that some level of fear was holding me back from stepping more boldly into my full radiance.

After a few more conversations with my own demons, I decided it's time to start being more generous in sharing my natural brilliance with the world.

It's time to start believing in miracles again.

miracle | mirik | | (noun)

~ a surprising and welcome event
that is not explicable by natural or scientific laws
and is therefore considered to be
the work of a divine agency

~a highly improbable or extraordinary event,
development, or accomplishment that brings
very welcome consequences

origin (Latin)

miraculum `object of wonder`

mirari `to wonder`... mirus `wonderful`

Creating Space for Miracles

There was a time in my story that I began to feel I might be over-using the word miracle.

I certainly don't want to make light of this beautiful word that many have reserved for a thing too precious to be spoken without an appropriate amount of reverence.

There's a special place in our language for words like wonder, awe, exquisite, and miracle, and I hope they will never be cast about heartlessly in ways that cause us to start taking them for granted.

Yet this word—miracle—keeps coming to mind, over and over, like a wave washing my awareness back into the ocean whenever my thoughts start to get stranded on dry land.

Pay attention to the miracle. Create space for miracles. Live in the miracle flow.

After years of following the whispers and allowing my inner knowing to lead me through layers of this complex concept that is more-than-a-word, I finally decided to look up the dictionary definition.

What a relief to know that the origin of this word is simply, *to wonder*. What a blessing that we might be granted a miracle by opening to the natural *wonder* of life, that we might begin to see the miraculous as we celebrate and witness the moments of simple *wonder* that surround us every day.

Perhaps the whole point of a miracle is the expansion of our hearts as we bow in pure, innocent wonder of what is beyond what we might have noticed, or believed, one moment before.

You might be thinking, *"So what is the point in looking for miracles when I'm barely managing to keep my head above water in my everyday life?"*

Well, that might be part of the reason. When we are so focused on 'managing' our busy-busy lives, it's easy to miss the wonder-full moments that are actually the essence of a life well lived.

Making space to fully receive those tiny yet miraculous moments is exactly what gives life its dimensionality. What a flat world it would be without our appreciation of the simple awe-inspiring miracles growing everywhere.

I'm a natural gardener, so it's easy to see why space is needed to grow anything. Even in compact gardens, each plant needs to be freed from weeds and given plenty of nourishment to grow into the best version of itself. I've seen way too many gardens left untended, and normally it's the weeds that win.

It's no different with life. If you crowd your days with too many meetings and too long to-do lists, you will likely miss seeing some of the small moments of wonder that are trying to squeeze their way into your life.

I recently experienced one of these nearly-missed miracle moments. I had decided I ought to be much busier making my business grow, so I filled my calendar with all the things I thought I was supposed to be doing, and before long I was so busy that I was barely managing to squeeze in a daily walk with my little dog, Emma Joy.

It was at the very beginning of one of these walks, as I was charging down the driveway...reading a text...barely noticing whether the sky was blue or grey, that I happened to look sideways instead of straight ahead. Something soft and furry next to the garage door caught my eye—a huddle of baby ducklings abandoned by their mother. (I later discovered the neighbor's dog had chased her away.) Thankfully, I found them when I did because they were growing weak from dehydration and lack of nourishment.

With a small bit of support, the ducklings eventually wandered back to their watery home, while I was left with a sweet memory and a reminder of everyday miracles.

It's a miracle *any* baby animal gets to survive the trials of growing up in nature. It can also be a miracle to wrap our hearts around a tender moment such as this.

My true miracle came after I realized how easy it would have been to miss the opportunity to give a bit of supply to someone(s) in need. I had a long 'list' of things I 'needed' to do that day, and it would have been very easy to walk right past this one. But the mother in me stepped in to put aside the list, attend to an obvious need, and give what was mine to give.

After I shifted my attention and slowed my pace to attend to those babies, I began to notice that I'd gotten a bit caught up in the creative flurry, and that I wasn't totally practicing what I'm teaching: slowing down to savor the simple miracles of life.

I wouldn't want to miss a miracle, would you?

Yes, I know there is much to do, and you're out there saving the world as best you can. I'm not suggesting you stop that (though I might show you some ways to do it without exhausting yourself). I'm not suggesting you move at a pace that feels sluggish to you. But if you're racing around with too many things on your list to notice when you're about to trip over one of life's wonders...you might just want to *stop-look-listen-breathe-sigh-gasp* and create a bit more space in your days.

When you begin to notice the everyday miracles, you will naturally give space for them to grow.

And once you start growing miracles, you may be surprised at how much happier your life is and how easy it is to move from barely surviving to thriving.

Then...if you'd truly like to grow a happier life, try planting a few miracles for others.

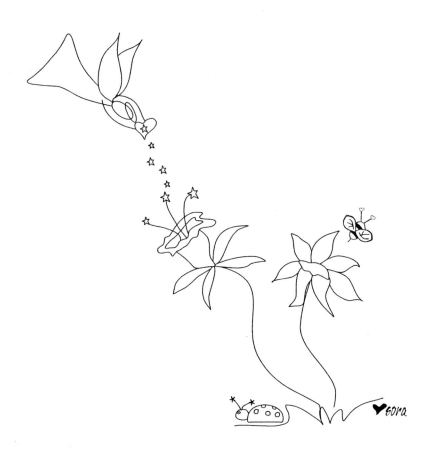

Recipe for Growing Miracles

Two wide open eyes

One willing grateful heart

A deep breath of AWE

Add a pinch (or two) of JOY

Sit in stillness for as long as it takes

Mix well with a heaping scoop of Generosity

(this recipe is best when shared)

Serve over and over.

Generosity: the Master Key

Sometimes it takes awhile for us to do the things we are called to do. I carried the first dream in a drawer of my mind for years before it began to emerge as the *Miracle Keys* story.

It took a second dream, along with quite a bit of courage and persistence, to share it with you. That dream came as a nightmare for a reason. It was meant to scare me out of complacency and into action.

If I would have listened the first time, I may not have needed that rather harsh nudge. But I'd left the story in a folder on my computer, and the idea to turn it into a book took a back seat to a thousand other things.

You see, I thought I was going to be writing a book about generosity and that it would look a bit more like a *normal* book with tips and tools for how to lead a more generous life.

I had no idea the *Miracle Keys* story was in me until I started writing; then I began having so much fun with the conversation that seemed to be writing through me that I couldn't stop!

But after the story was mostly written, I started thinking that it might not be understood...that it wasn't complete enough...that I needed to write the *real* book that's waiting in another corner of my mind.

After months of writer's block, and then the nightmare, I decided I'd better listen to the message from my first 'conversation' with the Angel.

The true miracle comes from sharing what lives in us—what flows naturally through us—with others.

While it might have been a lot of fun for me to write that story, it's not very generous of me to keep it all to myself, right?

Well, guess what?

The Miracle Keys IS a story about generosity. It's about unlocking your big bright heart and shining your love into the world more completely than you ever thought you could.

The truth about generosity is that it has more to do with fully receiving what we've already been given—then allowing that natural abundance to flow through—than it has to do with giving from any kind of material abundance.

Generosity is more a *way of being* than an *act of giving*, and there is nothing more bountiful than sharing our natural gifts.

So what is inside that big bright heart of yours, and how can you shine it even more generously into your world?

When you pay attention to a few simple things, you'll discover that it's really not that difficult to be generous. It's just a matter of finding what is yours to give, then making an ongoing commitment to give it with all your heart.

The first, and most important, *simple thing* is to pay close attention to what makes you happy. It might be anything—sitting silently watching a sunset, listening to a baby's laughter, walking by the ocean, or climbing the tallest mountain you can find. This is mostly about nourishing yourself with positive thoughts, which will open your cells so they can receive even more happiness. *(Do this often, at least once every day.)*

The next *simple thing* is to consider what you love to do that makes others happy. This is the part that's easy to forget in our mostly me-centered world, and it's the secret to finding lasting happiness. *(You'll believe me after you've tried it for a while.)*

Even noticing what you love that brings happiness is a good start, though you might also make a list to see if there are any common themes. Then you can follow those to create a life you love that is filled with what makes you and everyone happy. *(It's a wonder this is still a secret.)*

And this brings us to the last *simple thing*—keep waking up and loving the completely unique story you are creating with your life by doing whatever you can to stay OPEN to the unfolding mystery. This opening is the invitation for miracles to flow, and the key to a generously happy life.

Still trying to balance

a life filled with laughter & wonder & love,

knowing that kind of life is going to baffle

most everyone she meets.

Brian Andreas

A Generously Happy Life

$\mathcal{T}$here's a scene in the movie, *Secondhand Lions*, where a salesman comes to the door bringing packets of seeds to sell. The bachelor-brothers are looking for something to do with their nephew, who has become their newest project, so they decide to plant a garden. They faithfully plant all the seeds in rows, carefully labeling each row with the name on the various packets they purchased from the traveling seed-man.

Every row has a sign denoting what is planted there: beans, peas, corn, squash, and tomatoes. However, when the seeds begin to grow, the nephew notices that all the plants look the same. What the uncles failed to notice when they were planting is that every packet contained exactly the same seeds. Their garden didn't have much variety, but it did produce exactly what was planted: a full crop of corn.

I watched that precious movie years ago and the memory of that funny scene stayed with me, popping in vividly as I was beginning to write this chapter. The message is clear: we get what we plant, and we may not even know what we are planting!

It's so obvious with gardening, but how many people yearn for a different life, yet are not willing to change anything about what they are sowing every single day?

What if you could grow a happier life by simply changing just a few of your daily habits?

The habits we form are like seeds. They keep us planting away from whatever the repetitive part of our brain thinks it needs to do to survive. And therein lies the problem: the brain is wired to survive, not thrive. Thriving is the specialty of the heart.

If you want to do more than survive this life, which will you choose to follow, your head or your heart?

It may seem like a no-brainer to answer, but it's not easy to override the survival responses of the brain to let the heart's bright knowing lead the way. It takes huge leaps of faith and un-learning many of the habits formed through years of being schooled that it's smarter to think than to feel.

We're not here to debate which of these is more important... (both)...but take a moment to consider which seed habits you have formed out of fear of survival, rather than with a conscious intention to thrive. Are any of your habits helping you develop and share your most precious gifts? If not, perhaps it's time to consider creating a few new ones.

Then, consider this.

What if your happiest life depends entirely on how many seeds of kindness you plant for others?

One thing I've noticed is that many people think generosity is about sharing what we already have, and that until we have "enough," it really isn't possible for us to be truly generous.

But if you look up the definition, you'll see there's something much more noble about generosity—that it's about living into our largeness as we practice being just a bit more kind, going a bit beyond the expected, and giving a bit more than might be necessary in any situation.

If you've ever had an abundant garden, you'll know that much of the joy comes through sharing the bounty with others. Seasoned gardeners always plant more seeds than they need to sustain their own pantry. A few for the birds, a few for the neighbors... the harvest is always a time of giving.

The happiest people understand this about life. For one thing, it's pretty much impossible to keep happiness to yourself. It blossoms naturally. It's also quite contagious, so when you start casting about seeds from your own happy heart, you are bound to cross-pollinate.

So, what does it take to cultivate a generously happy life?

Your answer will be different from mine (or anyone else's), but once you find *your* "happy," the important thing is to "give more of it than expected" away.

Don't worry, it will be easy and you'll end up even happier once you get what this part is all about.

Once there was a girl who

wanted to CHANGE the world

& at first she thought it'd be easy,

because if everyone could see

how BEAUTIFUL it'd be,

it'd take about a minute.

But all the people she talked to

were too busy busy busy busy

to stop & listen. So she went off

& did beautiful things all on her own,

until pretty soon people were stopping & asking

if they could come along and Do That, too

& that's how she figured out how worlds change.

Brian Andreas

Finding Your Miracle Flow

*I*t's been years since I stopped trying to change the world. Until I discovered the real way worlds change, which is pretty much exactly like Brian Andreas says in that last quote.

Perhaps it's as simple as this: wake up each day, open your eyes, look around you (look truly & deeply), be grateful. Then find something to love & love it with every part of you.

Be willing to see a miracle in the simplest of moments. Let yourself be amazed by kindness. Find the place where joy resides in you and sit there awhile.

It's easy to find awe when you know how to look—through fresh innocent eyes that grow new every single day. The eyes of a child, before s/he has grown bored from being fed too much outer stimulation. The eyes you see through when you're just beginning to fall in love. Heart-connected eyes that see the sparkles in music, feel the colors of a rainbow. A poet's eyes.

This is the kind of seeing that is forgotten as we move through life on auto-pilot, eyes glazed over from looking at life through me-centered glasses, or through a filter of pain. We become immune to wonder, caught in the virus of just keeping up with the escalating speed of life.

It doesn't have to be this way.

What if, rather than life being a personal journey to accumulate all the desires and dreams we find along the way, life is more a treasure hunt, and *you* are the treasure?

What if every experience is simply an opportunity to unlock your personal treasure chest, not only for yourself, but for others to discover some of this bright bounty you hold inside?

What if you let go of every notion that you are here to change the world or receive anything at all for yourself and instead allow your time on earth to be spent purely in pursuit of shining your bright beacon heart by simply loving what you love...then joyfully sharing with everyone who comes your way.

Life is an ongoing awakening, and when we learn we are not here to receive anything, but to give more of what we have inside than we ever thought possible, life becomes an ongoing discovery. Miracles will find you.

This is the flow state—the place where giving and receiving are the same, where synchronicity is natural, where your natural gifts pour through to meet a certain need that you might not even have known was there.

This is how life is meant to be, and it's what happens when we give up the struggle to do what we think we are supposed to do and begin allowing our heart to lead the way.

If you haven't yet found the flow point of your life, if you're still struggling to hear your heart's rhythm over the strong beat of external voices, you might begin by practicing the Keys from part one.

Once you begin using those inner Keys—consistently and for the rest of your life (yes, you'll need them forever)—then you are ready to be a Key for the world.

Can you imagine a world where every single human has found their inner treasure and is sharing it abundantly with others?

I can, and it's a world rich beyond measure.

I see you doubt the parts of you

that love the world so much

you wonder if you'll ever

be able to show it

I want to take your face in

my hands & say, You who love

the world so much?

That's what you are here to do.

Brian Andreas

Remember Your Keys

*S*ometimes we cannot find what is right in front of our eyes—glasses, car keys, perhaps that double rainbow you failed to notice because you were looking down instead of up.

Other times we forget what we have promised to remember—a special moment engraved on the heart, one that made you feel everything was going to be fine no matter what happened from this point on.

So in case you forget your keys and would like a handy summary for the times you need to shift back into your miracle flow, here are a couple reminders.

The Forgiveness Key. Use it every time your mind turns toward the past (or future). This key will unlock the true gift of being present. (Remember that every-thing-is-for-giving, not keeping.) Forgiveness is not only about pardoning another (or yourself) and letting go of things that are no longer serving. It's also about opening your heart to the moment and being willing to give everything (even the good parts) to the great mystery.

The Laughter Key. Use this key a lot, multiple times every day. The laugh is what opens the door to the unlimited, returns you to a state of innocence, and frees your cells so they can breathe. (This key is especially helpful when you are feeling the weight of the world on your shoulders, though you may have to take some deep breaths of awe and gratitude before you can even find it.)

The Belief Key. "Believe you have something important to give, then give it with all your heart." Remember to turn off your mind beliefs so you can find what is real, then dive into your heart's bright knowing and trust the journey. Let faith be your guide.

The Gratitude Key. Never put this key down. It's the one that will help you find all the others when you've lost your way, especially when you feel it deeply. Remember, "when gratitude is deeply felt, it cannot help but overflow."

The Stillness Key. Return to this space to find every other key. You can do this anywhere, even in the middle of a busy shopping center. (Yes, really. It's about finding the still point within.) When you need a bit of help, try doing some deep breathing. Receive a deep breath, all the way into your belly. Hold for a moment. Feel the stillness of no breath. Now give this breath you have fully received with a burst of Hahhhhhhhh. Feel it reverberate through your body as you smile into the quiet space where all breaths meet—the place we are One.

A Final Angel Whisper

Dear Miraculous & Magnificent You,

I hope you enjoyed reading The Miracle Keys as much as I enjoyed writing it.

It's easy to put our dreams on hold while we attend to the ongoingness of life. It isn't always easy to create space and make time to follow the urges that arise when we finally stop to listen.

Yet this is how we follow our dreams—and how we become a miracle for others—by showing up and continuing to do one simple thing at a time to keep moving our love into the world.

Before this book was born, I was guided to create a way to help people keep opening to the ongoing wonder of life at the same time we join forces to create some real change for our world. It was a small thing I could do to inspire change.

And, in its own simple way, the *Everyday Miracle Network* has created small waves of love and generosity to ripple out from the circle of influence that begins with me.

I used to think I wasn't making a difference unless there was a huge wave of change that I could measure. Now I believe that the only lasting change comes in these tiny ripples of goodness that permeate one single heart at a time.

I invite you to be part of this miracle ripple and generosity movement at www.TheMiracleNetwork.net, where you will learn how to join an online Miracle Circle or receive resources to start one in your own communnity. As you gather with other believers to focus on celebrating the everyday heroes in our world, perhaps you'll find a few miracles in your own life just waiting to be revealed.

Wherever you are in your journey, may you find deep happiness and lasting abundance by cherishing the simple gifts and everyday miracles of being genuine, generous you!

-Shining Sor'a (Star, Idaho)

Gratitudes

I have a vision-partner who is one of my special angels. She was the one who initially 'saw' this book waiting in my aura and invited me to start writing again. She said it would come easily and be different than anything I had ever written. She was right. Thank you, Vasi Huntalas, for being a fresh-creative breath of wind that keeps guiding me to spread these wings.

Another angel—at least part inspiration for the one who spoke to me in my dreams—is my beloved spiritual teacher, Annam (Elle Re). Her guiding Presence has taught me more than I could ever capture in a book. So I do my best to keep writing the book of my life in gratitude for what flows generously through this embrace and embodiment of divine Word we know as Annam.

My creatively gifted friend, Jennifer Andrews, has once again shared her design talent with me. I appreciate the way she turns my ideas into a form that captures the essence of what I write.

Then there's Brian Andreas. I didn't go searching for his StoryPeople quotes. They were simply here, like another set of wings, waiting to punctuate my story with an infusion of his. And there was the magical way we were introduced by our mutual friend, Lynne Pallazzolo, just as I was trying to find him for permissions. That was another miracle. Thank you, Brian, for every part of that big wide creative heart you share with the world. I am beyond grateful.

(You can find Brian's famous line of StoryPeople art products at: www.StoryPeople.com)

Thank you to the early readers who encouraged me to turn the initial story into a book, and especially to Kevin and Stephanie Mullani @ Tru Publishing for encouraging me to follow my heart when choosing which book idea I wanted to finish (first).

And to Aspen Morrow @ Pottenger Press for helping me decide on a few of the finising pieces to move this book into the world, and most especially for connecting me with my brilliant cover designer, Sarah Bradbury of Silver Signet Graphic Design. I am thrilled with the way she captured the essence of this book.

Last (and equally important) thank you & you & you for reading the book all the way to the gratitude section. I write for myself, but also with a deep seed of trust that these words are inspiring others too.

End Note

Sor'a Garrett lives in Star, Idaho, with her husband of 37 years and an adorable mini-schnauzer named Emma-Joy...and in hugging distance from her highly creative daughter, artist-builder son and precious-amazing grandson. She sees life as an ongoing miracle, and she spends much of her time simply witnessing life's blessings through her writing and other forms of inspiration.

After a mostly happy and fulfilling career with a major high-tech company, Sor'a has been following her heart on a journey through educational innovation, spiritual non-profit leadership, and as a philanthroprenuer. She is happiest when she's creating, connecting, and being a catalyst for a more compassionate world.

You can find her through her website or on Facebook, where she is always delighted to connect with other believers.

Also by Sor'a & available on her website.

Silent Grace: a Celebration

Best of SHINE E-Book series:
Reveal your Brilliance
In the Garden of your Magnificence
Lighting the Splendid Torch

Believe in Miracles

To connect with the author,
visit her website @ SoraGarrett.com

or connect with her on Facebook: Sora Garrett

To create a Miracle Circle in your community, or
to become an online Miracle Activator,
come into our miracle playground @ TheMiracleNetwork.net

Book reviews can bring miracles too ...
Give yours @ Amazon.com